Cricut Projects

~

A Beginner's Guide to Mastering Your Cricut Machine

Table Of Contents

Introduction

Congratulations on purchasing this book, and thank you for doing so! I highly recommend reading the machine's user's manual first before reading this book. This way you know what I'm talking about in this book.

In the following chapters, you will be introduced to a variety of different tips, tricks, and techniques on how to get more out of your Cricut machine. As a beginner, it is important to learn the basics of how Cricut works and what materials work best for them. This will make creating projects much easier!

After all, is not everything easier when you know how to use it? Once you learn these basics, dive further into projects, both common projects, and some out-of-the-box ideas. Finally, gather some tried-and-true techniques to make using your Cricut a fun and easy crafting experience.

Do you need to give someone a gift this year? How about several people? Tired of giving the same, old gift card in a store-bought, generic card? Use your new Cricut to spice things up this year! Use this book to help you learn how to personalize gifts and create customized designs. But this life-changing machine is not just for you to make things for other people. Spice up your home with customized décor at a fraction of the cost it would be to buy it from the store, including things like prints, paper flowers, and etched glass or mirrors.

Components of the Cricut

When Cricut was introduced, it gave the world the desired tool for DIY projects in an easy, beautiful, and fun way. It changed the way creative's approached making projects and designing creations. It encourages passion and creativity. It makes people happy!

Any time, any place the magic of DIY can occur. The Cricut allows people from all over the world to find their own individualism. It provides the technique for professional creators or those new to DIY. The process is easy. Design the project, let the machine cut it out, and then smile at the beauty you have just created!

Model Overview

Listed from new to older versions.

Cricut Maker

This newest model, the Cricut Maker, is the ultimate machine. Just about 'anything' can be created thanks to its flexibility and diversity. A variety of materials can all be cut with precision.

Some of the newest features include:

- Applications improved for ease of use and designs can be saved.
- Precision and simplicity improved with the included washable fabric pen.
- Database of several hundred sewing patterns.
- Cut through up to 2.4 mm thick material with X-ACTO® knife-like precision using the Cricut Knife Blade™, which is being released in 2018.
- Slice through thick fabrics using the Cricut Rotary Blade™.

Cricut Explore Air 2™

A Machine built for speed! Compared to its older siblings, this machine is almost twice the speed. Over 100 different materials can be used.

Some of the features include:

- Big library of images and previously prepared projects to choose from.
- Create anywhere with compatibility for phones, tablets, and computers.
- Wireless cutting available with Bluetooth®.
- Settings for materials are easily adjusted using the Smart Set® function.
- Tool holder that can hold two tools at once minimizes the need for cutting and then writing or scoring.
- Exact cutting on a selection of materials with the technology, Cut Smart®.

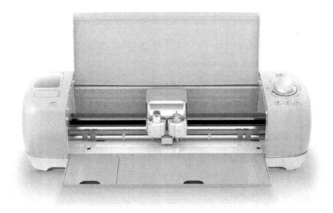

Cricut Explore Air

One of the first machines to successfully cut just about any material; from leather to paper and a multitude of options in between, the Cricut Explore Air introduces an electronic method for accomplishing intricate projects.

Some of the features include:

- Materials, from leather to adhesive, can be easily cut. Over 60 materials are known to work successfully with this machine.
- Applications designed for iPad tablets and developed online software for computers both provides Cricut Design Space™ is for free for users.
- The ability for personal images to be uploaded for free.
- Incorporated storage parts.

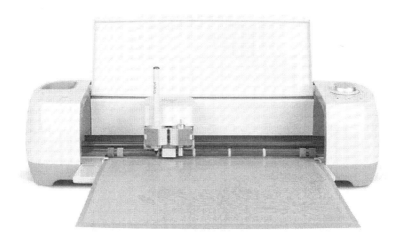

Cricut Explore One

The original Cricut machine, the Cricut Explore One, is the first of its kind. The accessible machine is affordable for almost everyone and gives novices and professionals alike access to the precise cutting. Great for a variety of DIY crafts and projects.

Some of the features include;

- Lowest price for a Cricut machine, making it one of the most affordable options.
- Precision cutting.
- Free fonts and the ability to upload personal images.
- A selection of provided images and projects to jumpstart creativity and make designing easier.
- Cutting mat and cutting blade made from German carbide are included.

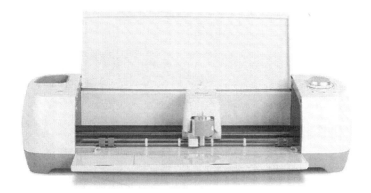

Tools

There are a variety of tools that can be purchased to compliment the Cricut, no matter the model that fits your lifestyle. Thankfully Cricut has compiled most of the essential tools into convenient sets, either to start off first-time Cricut users with the necessities or for special projects, like crafting and sewing.

If purchasing a toolset is not the path you wish to take, the tools can be bought separately. In addition, there are other tools that can be bought that are not in a kit. Below is a list of kits and tools with a short explanation of their various purposes.

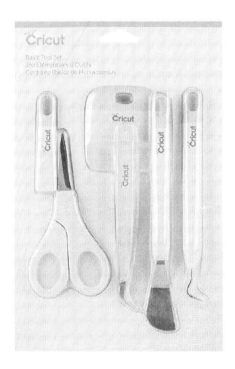

Tool Kits

Basic Tool Kit

All the 5 essential tools in one stop;

- Scraper to clean and polish
- Spatula to lift
- Micro-tip scissors
- Weeder
- Tweezers

Basics Starter Tool Kit

Another set of essential tools including;

- Scraper and spatula
- Point pens in metallic
- Scoring stylus
- Deep Cut Housing and 1 blade

Essential Tool Kit

Made for Cricut Explore models, this 7-piece set includes;

- Trimmer and replacement blade
- Scoring stylus
- Scraper for cleaning and polishing
- Spatula
- Micro-blade scissors
- Weeder
- Tweezers

Paper Crafting Tool Kit

This 4-piece set is perfect for professional paper crafting and includes;

- Craft mat
- Distresser for edges
- Quilling tool for spirals
- Piercer for small piece placement

Sewing Tool Kit

Sewing essentials are all in one place. This set includes;

- Thimble made of leather
- Measuring tape
- Pins and pin cushion
- Seam ripper
- Thread snips
- Fabric shears

Weeding Tool Kit

A set of 5 tools for elaborate cutting and vinyl DIY crafts includes;

- Hook tweezers
- Fine tweezers
- Hook weeder
- Weeder
- Piercer

Complete Starter Tool Kit

Perfect for the beginning Cricut user, this set includes;

- Black window cling
- Cutting mat
- Point pens in metallic
- Scoring stylus
- Deep Cut Housing and 1 Blade
- Scraper to clean and polish
- Spatula to lift
- Micro-tip scissors
- Weeder to remove negatives
- Tweezers

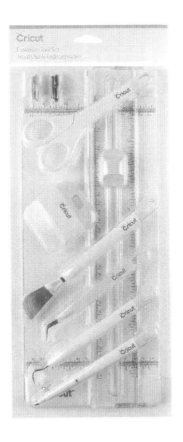

Single Tools

XL Scraper
Clean mats quickly and easily adhere sizeable projects to an assortment of surfaces with this tool. Great for vinyl and can be used with all Circuit models.

Portable Trimmer
Precision cutting is achieved with the 15-inch swinging arm, and the storage for a replacement blade makes this an extra-functional tool. Swiftly insert materials, cut, and measure from both directions with the dual-hinged rails.

Scoring Stylus
3-dimensional projects, boxes, card, and envelopes' lines can be scored in 1 step with this tool that holds the blade for cutting and the stylus. This tool is best for Cricut Maker and Explorer models.

Applicator and Remover
Remove or apply textiles easily and make the cutting mat last longer with these functional tools. Ideal for the Cricut Maker, these tools are sold together to make working with fabric that much easier.

Brayer

This roller made of soft rubber applies materials smoothly to a variety of surfaces. Ideal for printmaking and with the Cricut.

Eliminate every last wrinkle, kink, bubble, and pucker with ease. The Cricut® Brayer firmly adheres material to your cutting mat and is perfect for pressing down fabric, vinyl, or iron-on, as well as inking blocks for printmaking.

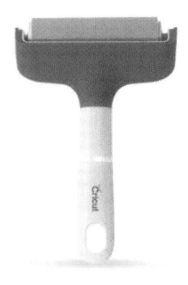

Scraper and Spatula

Lift and clean easily with these two tools. Made especially for the cutting mat for all sorts of projects.

Scissors

Make clean cuts with micro-tip scissors, and store them safely with the included end cap and cover for the blades.

Tweezers

Secure project pieces after lifting them with the reverse-grip of this tool. Perfect to use for little items like small cuts and intricate trimmings.

Weeders

Use this tool to remove small cuts and for separating iron-on pieces and vinyl from their liners.

Accessories

Similar to the tools available for the Cricut, there are also a variety of accessories that can be purchased to compliment whatever model of Cricut you choose. Below is a list that highlights some of the available accessories and their functions. Consider purchasing them individually or take advantage of the different bundles and sets offered.

Functional Support Accessories

Specially designed accessories are made to enhance the experience of using a Cricut machine with function and style.

Mats

- Light grip
- Standard grip
- Strong grip
- Fabric grip

Scoring and Blades

- Rotary blade
- Fabric blade- bonded
- Deep cut blade
- Fine-point blade
- Premium blade made of German carbide
- Scoring stylus

Pens

- Variety of colored pens
- Extra fine tip colored pens
- Ultimate fine tip colored pens
- Fabric pen that is washable
- Variety of colored markers

Tape

- Glitter tape

Adapters and Tech

- Cartridge adapter
- Pen adapter
- Bluetooth adapter
- Accessory adapter
- USB cable
- Power cord
- Keyboard overlay

For the crafter on the go or in need of stylish and functional storage, these accessories are the perfect fit.

Pouches

- Accessory pouches for tools

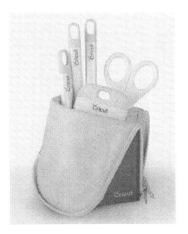

Totes and Bags

- Crafters shoulder bag
- Rolling crafters tote
- Machine tote

Machine Add-On's

Cricut machines can accomplish many great things, but sometimes they could use a sidekick. That's where these machines come in.

Easy Press
Achieve the iron-on results like a professional in less than a minute! Simple to use and light to carry, this accessory is the perfect for Cricut users who want t-shirt transfers to last.

Easy Press Bundles:
- Bulk
- Ultimate
- Everything

Cuttlebug

Cut or emboss almost any material on the run with this handy machine. Achieve the professional, clean cuts you want with ease.

Cuttlebug Add-on's:
- Mats
- Dies
- Materials
- Spacer plates
- Cutting mats

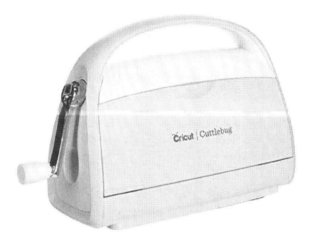

Bright Pad

This durable, light pad offers a soft, adjustable light to make tracing, cutting, and easier and more comfortable on the eyes.

Sets

Basic

Perfect for the Explore machines, this set includes spatula and scraper tools, a pen set, a stylus for scoring, and a deep cut blade with its housing.

Ultimate

An enhanced set of accessories for the Explore machines, this set includes black window cling, 3 different cutting mats, a pen set, a stylus for scoring, and a deep cut blade and its housing. It also includes the basic toolset which contains spatula and scraper tools, scissors with a blade cover, a weeder, and tweezers.

Explore Air 2 black + ultimate package - $270

Cricut Access

To maximize the possibilities with the different machines, Cricut offers a service called "Access." This membership has different levels and unique benefits such as discounts and member-only access to design services. Three different Access memberships are listed below with a brief explanation of each one.

Fonts

Hundreds of fonts, some that non-members cannot access, are available in the most affordable Access membership, Fonts. It can cost as little as $5 per month, and it is not a contract, meaning at any time you can cancel the membership.
Limitations include that they are only to be used with Explore and Maker machines and the fonts do not include licensed fonts, like Disney.

Standard

A more comprehensive Access membership, Standard, offers even more exclusive access and benefits. Any purchase on Cricut.com and Design Space is 10% off, and the database includes over 30,000 images, many of which are not available for non-members. It also includes the same benefits as Fonts, including the ability to cancel when needed. The cost for this membership is about $8 per month.

The limitation of this membership is that it does not include many licensed cartridges, fonts, or images such as Disney, Sesame, or Sanrio Hello Kitty products. This is probably a good package to go with if you are starting out.

Premium

The most comprehensive Access membership, Premium, combines the benefits of Fonts and Standard memberships and adds on more. Additional cartridges, images, and fonts are up to 50% in Design Space. Free shipping is also offered for orders with a total over $50. For a yearly fee of about $120 ($10 a month), it includes access to over 1,000 projects.

One limitation, like the other memberships, is that Premium does not have access to many licensed cartridges, images, and fonts and the 50% discount cannot be applied to purchase of these items. The discounts also cannot be used with other promotional offers.

Cartridges

This unique feature of the Cricut allows anyone accesses to professional images and fonts for whatever they desire to create. Professional to novice crafters can enjoy the versatility of the cartridges easily. The range of cartridges offered fit just about any need you may have, and one cartridge offers a variety of ideas within its theme. Simply insert the cartridge into your machine and link it to your Cricut account online to use the images and fonts. Create the perfect designs for whatever occasion! You can order cartridges online too.

Some of the cartridges available are listed below.

Licensed characters and themes

- Disney
- Sanrio
- Boy Scouts
- Marvel
- Wordsworth
- Teresa Collins

Specially designed for cards

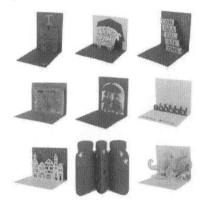

- Holiday, Birthday and Thank you cards
- Special card designs such as pop-up designs, box cards, and everyday themes

Events

- Weddings
- Birthdays
- Babies
- Graduations
- Anniversaries

Seasons

- Spring
- Summer
- Fall

- Winter

Holidays

- Christmas
- Hanukkah
- Easter
- Thanksgiving
- New Year's
- Mother's and Father's Day

Perfect for every day

- Home décor images and fonts
- Sports images and fonts
- Religious images and fonts

- Children related images and fonts such as animals, school, and toys

Special fonts

- Disney fonts
- Varsity fonts
- Holiday-themed fonts
- Themed fonts
- Non-English fonts such as American Sign Language, the Greek alphabet, and Hebrew

Projects and Materials

Certain materials can be cut on various Cricut machines, but it does vary from machine to machine. The newer machines have more functionality with more materials. No matter the machine though, there are some materials you may have thought of, like those listed on the Cricut's website, while there are others you may not have thought of. Just like you may not have thought of some out-of-the-box ideas for projects to do!

Materials Listed on Cricut.com
Cricut.com is a treasure-trove of information for both the new and experienced Cricut user. One helpful feature is the list and store for materials. The items listed for sale on the website include:

- Cling for windows
- Washi sheets
- Vinyl
- Vellum
- Transfer Tape
- Poster board
- Iron-on materials
- Foils
- Leather-like materials
- Craft foam
- Papers, including cardstock.

Within these categories, multiple items are also listed. For example, under vinyl, items are included like basic vinyl, transfer vinyl, and adhesive vinyl. Ultimately, the Cricut website lists over 100 different materials that the machines can cut, many of which they sell on the site. This is very convenient if you want to guarantee the materials will work with the machine and you do not want to waste their time shopping around for things.

Other people prefer to try more out-of-the-box materials and projects to test their creative powers and those of their machines.

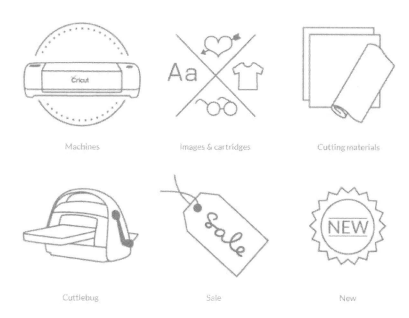

Machines   Images & cartridges   Cutting materials

Cuttlebug   Sale   New

Alternative Materials

While vinyl is one of the most popular materials to cut with your Cricut, that material is just the "tip of the iceberg," so to speak. There are so many other materials crafters have used successfully with their Cricut machines. Below is a list of some of the items to consider;

Balsa Wood
Balsa is a quick growing, American tree. The thin wood it produces is often used in model making or rafts. This is because it is very lightweight and slightly pliable. Craft projects from balsa wood include favor tags for wedding or parties, rustic-looking placeholders for the table, or a natural-themed sign for a door or wall

Pens

While this is not exactly an unusual material, it is an often under-used tool. These pens can not only be functional but beautiful.

Some projects a pen can be used for include creating adult coloring pages, placemat designs for children at restaurants or holidays (of course, these are great for adults, too!), or monogrammed jewelry. For example, a metallic initial can be printed on a circular piece of leather and strung on a necklace for an instant, personal statement piece of jewelry.

Duct Tape

The popularity of duct tape as a fashion or crafting item has blossomed over the past few decades, producing projects from wallets to prom dresses. It is still a material that some Cricut DIY-ers underestimate.

This material can be durable and fashionable. Projects made using Duct Tape include Bold and textured gift tags for packages or an art portfolio that showcases the vibrancy and precision of the artist with the added touch of this material.

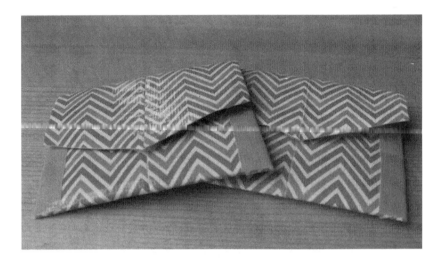

Fabric

Fabric is not an unusual material for some Cricut users, but because the variety of fabric available to choose from is so vast, it needs to be mentioned again because there are some techniques and materials that are a little more unusual. For example, cutting a lace-like pattern into fabrics can immediately add a color-palette of fancy lace to any project. This also makes it possible to have the same lace pattern on a variety of complimentary fabrics or colors.

Faux Leather and Leather

Cricut.com does not sell real leather. They offer a variety of different leather-like or "faux" leathers. "Faux" means "fake."

Depending on your preference, you can use either material. Despite what you choose, both are good materials to cut in the Cricut. Custom jewelry, like necklace pendants or earrings, are simple and stunning projects. These make beautiful and personal gifts or add the right touch to a special outfit. Leather can also be used for making fashionable bracelets or cuffs.

Having an intricate cut on a lovely piece of leather or faux leather, the bracelet can be attached to an adjustable band. Hair bows or bows to add to clothing or handbags are also possible. For a hair bow, hot glue a hair clip to the back when the bow is finished. Use hot glue or another adhesive to attach the bow to clothing or a purse. Other hair accessories can be made, like flowers and other shapes.

These can be attached to hair clips, like the bows, or attached to hard or stretchy headbands. Leather can also be used as an embellishment to pillows or other fabrics, like chair backs, or made into manly coasters.

Felt

Felt is another multi-functional material that creative's can use for a host of projects. Because this item is fairly sturdy but has good flexibility, it is perfect for just about anything.

In addition, it comes in all different colors and is relatively inexpensive. Some unique projects that can be made from felt include garlands of multi-layered flowers to hang over a window curtain or above a bed, a textured phrase attached to a pillow, an interactive tree-shaped advent calendar, banners, ornaments, and cupcake or cake toppers.

Magnets

Magnets can be used for more than just the fridge, and thankfully the Cricut is there to help create new and fun ways to make magnets for all these different purposes. Be selective about the type of magnet you choose to cut.

Thick and solid magnets do not work well for these projects, but the thinner sheets of magnets are good for fun crafts.

Some ideas that are outside the fridge-box include; a magnet to be attached to the dishwasher that indicates if the machine is loaded with dirty or clean dishes, magnetic busy boards such as a mermaid scene with underwater characters or a race track with cars and spectators (do not forget a trophy for the first across the finish line!). Magnetic words to spell out messages on the side of the car or, yes, on the fridge, or school pride or mascots to attach to the car.

Cling for the window

Custom decals for holidays or to create a statement on the car or a mirror can cost a lot of money if it is bought from a store or ordered custom from a shop.

Instead, use your Cricut to get crafty. Consider making a saying or image and stick it to the window.

Leather Keychain

This may not be considered a particularly wild project, but leather key chains can be pricey. Thankfully Cricut has an answer. Use the key fob template in Design Space and choose one from the designs.

Set the Smart Dial to Leather and load a pen if personalization is being added as well. Initials or special dates are great for this project. Press "Go."

Once the leather is cut, determine where rivets will be placed and use the Piercer tool to poke holes in the leather for the base of the rivet to fit through. If you are not using a design with a rivet, a simple stitch may be required.

Still, use the Piercer to poke holes where the stitch will be. After the rivet or stitch is complete, add the key ring, close the rivet with a tap from a mallet or glue and allow to dry overnight.

Tablet Case

Another project that can save a lot of money and provide a custom touch is a tablet case. Using Design Space, cut two rectangles of fabric. Leather is a good material for this, but any sturdy and non-scratchy material will do.

One rectangle should have a half circle cut at the top in the middle to help get the tablet in and out. If personalizing, choose a design to draw onto the top of the rectangle that has the half circle removed. Once the pieces have been cut and drawn on, place them together, with the right sides or fashion sides facing out and stitch around the edges to attach them together. If sewing is not a strong suit, a thin line of glue can be used. Keep in mind that extra width will be needed depending on how you attach the front and back together.

Custom Bedding and Pillows

Creating custom shaped pillows is one way to customize bedding, but another way it to create custom add-ons to other pillowcases, sheets, and bedspreads. For example, adding monograms or images onto the pillowcases with vinyl or stencils and fabric paint are great methods.

Match a custom theme in a room with images ironed on to a bedspread or duvet cover and match the image on corresponding pillowcases. This means you can purchase bedding as inexpensively as you wish and provide the perfect matching details to round out a room. Children's bedding is another good place for this customization. Consider doing a custom shaped throw pillow, with matching pillowcases in a coordinating theme and a matching bedspread all for a fraction of the cost this custom set would cost you at a store.

Diamond Shaped Hanging Planter
Creating a beautiful vase or basket is a great way to save money and grow plants or store items in style. Using the Cricut, chipboard, glue, and paint, this planter can easily be added to any room. To hang the planter, add a leather cord to the list of supplies.

Begin by creating the diamond design and uploading it to Design Space. A suggested size is to create 6 of the lower triangles, 2.3 inches wide X 2.82 inches, and 6 of the upper trapezoid, 2.3 inches wide X .76 inches. It is advisable to cut a few extra to be safe. When ready to cut, set the Smart Dial to "Custom" and choose "Chipboard Heavy- 0.7 mm" and press "Go." After completing the first cut, do not remove the project or move the mat. Press "Go" again.

After the materials are cut, glue them together with the 6 triangles on the bottom and the 6 trapezoids on the top. A strip of tape can help hold these together as they dry.

Same applies to assembling the triangle/trapezoid shapes into the final diamond shape. Use hot glue to seal all the diamond seams. If wanting to hang the planter, punch 2 holes on opposite sides. Do not string the leather through yet. First, paint the planter whatever color you desire and allow it to dry. This sometimes requires more than one coat. Once done painting, add the leather cording, if you are using it.

Because these are not waterproof, either fill with faux plants or place a small waterproof container on the inside and plant the flower in that. Adding small gravel, like fish tank gravel, can add a nice touch and cover up the container inside the hanger.

Even if using faux plants, the small gravel is a nice touch. For storage, this hanging planter can hold a variety of items because of the strength of the leather; however, keep in mind that the planter is made from chipboard. Do not overload the planter with too many heavy things to prevent it from breaking apart.

It's best to choose succulents for this because they do not require much water.

It is important to realize that the Cricut is not just another cutting machine. It can do the basic function of cutting letters and making iron-ons, but as the previous part of this chapter highlighted, there is so much more it can do.

For those that may still be using the older models of the Cricut, it is worth considering an upgraded machine because the abilities are more advanced.

The newer models offer a larger number of benefits. You still get the function of the older models and other cutting machines but the drawing and cutting have become more precise, and the materials it can cut have expanded. It also opens up the possibility for more of the unique projects, some of which you may have never thought of before.

How to Use the Cricut

Setting Up the Machine

The first step in the process of setting up a Cricut is to determine where the machine will be best located. Ideally, the machine will be placed near a computer or tablet, a power source and where it has room to work. Even if the machine does not require to be hooked to a computer, try to keep it within reach to make the process of loading and unloading easier.

Spacing around and above the machine should also be considered. A minimum of 10 inches to the front and back is ideal for the mats to move around as needed. The space in front of the machine should be flat and level with the machine, so the mats lay flat. If the mats are not flat some materials, do not work well, and when the mats are unloaded, they will fall to the floor, potentially damaging the mat. A folding table in front of the machine can be a solution. If this is not an option and you must choose between the location to the computer and a flat surface, choose to be closer to the computer. A minimum of 12 inches above the machine is desired so tools can be inserted under the lid easily.

The installation of a newer Cricut machine can be done in minimal steps. After the completion of all the installation steps you will start out a free trial of Cricut Access, which gives access to additional projects, images.

To begin:

1. Turn on the machine after it is connected to the power source.
2. Use Bluetooth or the USB cable to connect the machine to the computer or your device.

To set up a Cricut on a Mac or Window's computer;

1. Go to the website for setup: https://design.cricut.com/setup
2. If you do not have a Cricut.com account, create one to log in, or use your account information to log into Cricut.com
3. When prompted, the Design Space plug-in should be downloaded and installed on the computer.
4. Cricut Access will ask for acceptance of the terms of use to activate the free trial.
5. When the prompt to make the first cut appears to set up is complete.

To set up a Cricut on an iOS device:

1. Visit the App store and download the Design Space app.
2. Create a Cricut.com account or log into your account once the app is launched and it prompts for the login.
3. Open the menu and tap "Machine Setup and App Overview."
4. Select "New Machine Setup."
5. Finish the set up by following the screen prompts.
6. When the prompt to make the first project appears to set up is complete.

If the machine does not get set up completely during the first time it is connected, in the Design Space account menu, go to "New Machine Setup," or visit cricut.com/setup after the machine is re-connected to the computer or device. Follow the prompts to complete the setup process.

Cricut Software

Design Space

Design Space is for any Explore machine with a high-speed, broadband Internet connection that is connected to a computer or an iOS device. This more advanced software allows full creative control for users with Cricut machines.

Craft Room

Some machines, such as the Explore and Explore Air, cannot use Craft Room, but many other models can. Craft Room users also have access to a free digital cartridge, which offers images that all Cricut machines can cut.

Cricut Basics

For new users, Cricut Basics is the ideal app. Without the more advanced features like in Design Space, Basic offers an easy and fast way to select and print a pre-made project, image, or font.

How to Use Design Space

To begin, choose a project that is simple. For example, select a pre-made design so practicing with the tools and functions is easier. Use the first couple of projects to learn how the software works before trying more challenging projects. Also, utilize the video tutorials on Cricut's website for additional help navigating how to use this tool.

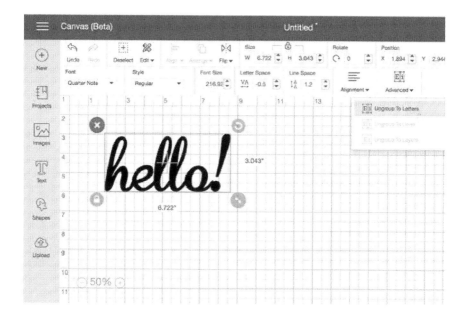

The first step in using the software is to open it. Select "Create New Project," and then "Image." In the following screen, an image list will appear. You may scroll through the list or type in keywords for what you would like to make. Try rephrasing what you are looking for if you do not see what you want.

When you like a project, look for the price to determine what you want to pay. Many are free, but some do have a cost. In addition, projects may be for cutting or printing. If they are a printing project, they will have the image of a printer in a circle tagged on the project. For this example, choose a project that is for cutting. Select the project you like and select "Insert."

The image is now in the workspace. This is the place for changes. In the beginning, try not to make any major changes. Once the changes are complete, the project is ready for cutting. Select the green "Make It" circle. Now the project moves to the cutting mat visual. It is advisable to look at the different mats that are needed and to line up paper and vinyl in the order of their cutting place. After reviewing and preparing, scroll back and click "Continue," another green circle.

When the cutting begins Design Space will provide prompts along the way of what to do. Follow the prompts quickly and accurately. If a tool is needed, the screen will prompt for it to be inserted. For example, if a stylus is required, open the lid, insert the stylus until it clicks and then close the lid. Move the dial onto the material required and then press the flashing buttons. Loading is indicated with the first flashing button, and cutting and scoring are indicated with the second flashing button. Remove the project from the mat when completed.

Introduction to Cutting

There are many materials a Cricut can cut. Vinyl is one of the most popular items people like to use. There is also a wide range of vinyl types, but Cricut claims there are over 100 types of materials the machine can cut. Some of the top materials include:

- Iron-on
- Paper
- Vinyl
- Fabric
- Plastic

Other items include crafting materials; like foam, paper with glitter, and Washi tape, and thick materials; like woods, leather, and magnets. Found materials are another option and are a less-expensive option. Some of the things people have used include aluminum from cans, cardboard from cereal boxes, and chipboard.

Testing Cuts

When beginning a project, always do a test cut on a scrap material. Do not use the final material, which is often more expensive and precious, in case there is a problem with the design. Try to choose a scarp material similar in weight and texture to your final material for accuracy.

Many people skip this step but end up regretting it when the material is ruined. Problems can include the cutting pressure is too hard and slices the mat, ruining the cutting mat, or at the very least, an extra cut may be required for success.

This process does not need to take a long time, but it can save a lot of time on the back end if a design mistake was made.

Cutting with fabrics

Fabric is a challenging medium to cut on for most Cricut machines, especially because there are so many types of fabric to choose from. This material usually requires much trial and error to discover what works best. Sometimes a material will cut fine while other times it will snag and drag over the cutting mat. A tip for working with fabric, particularly thin fabrics, is to use a bonding material to be adhered to the fabric to make it thicker and sturdier. If bonding is not an option, at least use a stiff interfacing to help. Again, test cuts are essential in all projects, but they are especially important when working with fabrics.

Cutting with Vinyl

After preparing and reviewing a project to be cut, when it is sent to the machine for cutting, make sure to adjust the machine's Smart Dial to the appropriate materials, for example, vinyl. Older machines may not have this material listed, and it is best to review tutorials online for suggestions on how to modify an older machine to work with this material. If working with iron-on vinyl, turn the "Mirror" switch on to ensure it prints correctly.

Select the mat that the vinyl will be cut on and adhere the vinyl to the mat, placing the paper located on the back of the vinyl facing down on the mat and put it in the machine to be cut. If there are multiple colors or vinyl's to be cut, gently peel the finished, cut vinyl from the mat and adhere the next piece. Weeding may be required for the background vinyl before attaching it to the project.

Cricut Projects

Stenciling

Stencils are a valuable DIY tool, especially for those that do not do well in designing images with their hand. But traditional, store-bought stencils can be expensive and the selection limited. Using the Cricut can be a more cost-effective and more customizable. The materials that work best for creating a stencil include vinyl and contact paper.

To accomplish this task, do not remove the paper backing from the contact paper or vinyl before placing it on the mat to be cut. Offsetting the vinyl slightly can assist in compensating for the backing being left on, and it ensures the cuts will be on the vinyl and not on the backing paper.

Use the adjustments below for blade depth and speed, pressure, and the number of cuts to ensure the material is the only thing cut and the backing is left intact.

Vinyl Made Just for Stencils

Cricut now makes vinyl that is designed just for creating stencils! In addition, helpful tips on machine setting adjustments are provided on their website but also provided below.

As mentioned previously, it is important that the machine does not cut through both the vinyl and the backing. The term for this type of cut is called "Kiss Cut." The material Cricut provides works similar to traditional vinyl, but like the previous vinyl mentioned, the backing is left on the vinyl when it is placed on the mat. After the mat is loaded into the machine, the settings must be manually adjusted to provide the "Kiss Cut" that is desired.

Once settings are adjusted, tell the machine to cut, and it should produce the correct result. Because machines and materials can vary, do not forget to do a test cut first to make sure it works before cutting the final material.

After the vinyl is cut out, use the "Weeding" hook tool to remove any remaining and unwanted items. Carefully remove the vinyl's backing and adhere it to the project. Use a scraper or a popsicle stick to rub or burnish the vinyl stencil onto the project to remove air bubbles. This process also ensures the vinyl is properly sealed to the project. Once satisfied with the adherence of the stencil, apply the paint or other substance to be used on the stencil, coating as often as needed. Let the project dry completely before removing the stencil.

"Kiss Cut" Adjustments for Stencil Vinyl

- Cricut Explore: Adjust the Smart Dial to "Custom" and select "Stencil Vinyl- 0.2 mm (Cricut)" from the list of materials created custom for Cricut and Explore machines.
- Cricut Mini: #3 blade depth, #2 pressure, high speed, 1 multi-cut, regular blade assembly.
- Cricut Imagine: #3 blade depth, #3 pressure, high speed, 1 multi-cut, regular blade assembly.
- Circuit Expression 2: #4 blade depth, #3 pressure, high speed, 1 multi-cut, regular blade assembly.
- Cricut Expression: #3 blade depth, medium pressure, high speed, 1 multi-cut, and regular blade assembly.
- Cricut Create: #3 blade depth, medium pressure, high speed, 1 multi-cut, and regular blade assembly.

Home Decor Ideas

The Cricut can be a useful tool for creating quality, easy and inexpensive home décor items. These items can be made completely from the machine or be used to add to items, like creating labels or accessories. Some of the main ways the Cricut can be used to create home décor includes wall décor, artwork, typography, accessories, and labels.

Wall Décor
Adding decals to the walls and surfaces of the home is a fast and inexpensive method for updating a space in a non-permanent way. This is also a wonderful method for adding a personal touch to a rented space such as an apartment or dorm room. Some popular wall décor projects include;

- "Tile" backsplash for behind the kitchen sink.
- Golden polka dots for a wall cover.
- 3-D paper flowers for above a crib or girl's bed.
- Bee decals for the backs of built-in bookcases

Artwork

Original artwork satisfies the need to cover the large expanses of wall, adding color and interest, and to bring life into a room. Using a Cricut to create your own art is a great solution that saves money and time. Some popular artwork ideas include:

- Cardstock chevron contemporary patterns in a frame.
- Silhouette of states that mean something to you.
- Magnetic memo board in the shape of the United States.
- Gallery frame with twine and clothespin to swap out "polaroid" style images.

Flower made with a cricut

Typography Artwork

Similar to other artwork projects, the purpose of typographical art is to add interest and customization to a space, but unlike shapes or images, these forms of artwork directly tell a person viewing it what to think. They can be playful, serious, or functional. Some popular typography artwork projects include:

- Golden phrases made added to wooden backgrounds.
- Plaques made with fun sayings, like "wash, dry fold" for a laundry room.
- Watercolor lettering. This is great for writing the alphabet for a modern children's room or playroom.

Accessories

Because the Cricut can cut a variety of materials, from leather to fabric, home accessories can be a great area for creativity. Also, the machine can be used to embellish already-owned or designed items, such as furniture, and vases. Some popular accessory projects include:

- Memo boards monogrammed with full initials or just the last name's initial.
- Dresser updated with vinyl details. This is excellent for updating a scuffed dresser or another piece of well-loved furniture.
- Pillow in various shapes, like hearts, stars and circles.

Labels

Some of the ways to update accessories are to add labels to them. Text and image labels can be very functional. For example, if a child is not reading yet but needs to know where to find and put clothing items, images of those items can be labeled onto the corresponding drawers to prevent constant frustration, both the child and the parent. Some popular label projects include:

- Toy bin labels with images.
- Bins in the laundry room labeled with cute images and texts for colors, whites, and delicates.
- Stakes to identify plants in the garden.

Personalized Gifts

There really is no shortage of crafts to be designed using the Cricut. No matter the personal preference or style of a friend, colleague, or family member, the Cricut can offer a way to make it even more special.

Some ideas for personalized gifts are;

- Teacher gifts, such as a custom pencil holder or coffee cup.
- Customized Christmas ornaments with images or names stenciled on to them.
- Frosted and personalized jars for candles or treats.
- Etched wine glasses with sayings or initials. This is also great for wedding gifts for the new Mr. and Mrs.
- Designed serving plates filled with treats.
- Monogrammed flower vase filled with a favorite plant or seeds.
- Sports-themed bean bags and boards for corn-hole or bags game.
- Personalized gift bags and boxes.

To get more inspiration for gift ideas, consider finding a source of inspiration on the Cricut website and Facebook page or on sites such as Pinterest. Once a gift idea is selected, purchase all the required materials. Consider what materials will be needed for the Cricut machine, such as vinyl or fabric, and what the rest of the project will need. For example, if creating a custom pencil holder for a teacher gift, the gift will also require a straw holder, number 2 pencils, and corresponding ribbon.

Once the materials are assembled, choose the design to be added to the holder. This can be a monogram or a teacher-related design. The inspirational photos and projects researched earlier can be a big help in this step. Create the design in Design Space and cut it out on vinyl. If it is a stencil, make sure to use a stencil vinyl and adjust the setting accordingly. Cut the design out and weed it before applying it to the holder. Fill the holder with the pencils and wrap a piece of the ribbon around the top, tying it into a bow.

The ribbon used can also be customized. For example, if a stencil is created in Design Suite, apply it to the ribbon and paint the custom design onto it, repeating as necessary to cover the length of ribbon desired. The teacher's name or the school name is a great addition. This works best for a wider ribbon. This also works very well for present wrappings for birthdays or holidays.

Another personalized gift is a custom-designed card. Design Space offers many free or low-cost card designs to choose from. The colors in the design are only suggestions, as it will depend on you what color cardstock you use in the project. Choosing to include a person's name or something special that they like on the card adds an extra level of personalization.

Consider choosing colors and themes that relate to the person you are giving the gift to. You can combine function and fun in one gift by carefully considering their needs and interests. For example, someone may need new glassware for their home, but they also love pineapples. Consider creating custom glassware with etched pineapples for a beautiful gift.

Decorating Clothing

To decorate clothing, two vital choices must be made. One is the decision of what is to be said or displayed on the clothing. For beginners, consider sticking to one-color designs. The second is to determine the kind of clothing the design will be placed on. T-shirts are great first projects.

One suggestion is to avoid clothing that says not to iron because it can end up being ruined if you try to iron on vinyl. Also, consider the stretch of the fabric. You will need to peel off the backings to the vinyl, which pulls on the clothing.

T-Shirt Design

To create a custom t-shirt, follow these instructions.

1. Choose an image.
2. Open Design Space. Press "Canvas" to open a new workspace. Choose a canvas that aligns with the type of project you will be doing, such as a t-shirt, and the size of the shirt.
3. Upload the design. Press "Upload an image" and look for the file of the image you have chosen. Identify the image's type. "Simple Cut" is the type of image most iron-on projects use.
4. Use the tools to select the interior of the image or text that will be cut out. For lettering, select the insides of each letter.
5. When finished, tell the computer to have the machine "Cut Image." Do not choose "Print then Cut Image."
6. When the item is on the canvas, adjust the measurements, if needed.
7. Prepare the vinyl for cutting by adjusting the Smart Dial to Iron-on and attaching the iron-on vinyl to the mat, placing the shiny side down.
8. Press "Cut."
9. Before hitting "Go," toggle the "Mirror" switch on.
10. When the cutting is finished, weed the design and cut away the extra vinyl. It is now ready to be attached to the t-shirt.
11. Turn on your iron and turn off the steam feature. Adjust the heat controls on the iron to the hottest setting it offers.
12. For about 15 seconds, warm up the t-shirt with the iron. This trick helps the vinyl adhere properly and easily.

13. Identify where on the t-shirt the design will be placed and lay the vinyl on that spot. Cover the vinyl with a clean piece of cotton material or a pressing cloth to prevent the plastic from melting onto the fabric.
14. Place the iron on top of the cotton pressing cloth for about 30 seconds. Turn the shirt over and press the back of the shirt where the image is located for another 30 seconds.
15. Flip the shirt back to the side with the vinyl and remove the pressing cloth and the sticky part from the vinyl. Do not wait until the project is cool! If a part of the iron-on is sticking to the backing, place the iron over that part for a few seconds and then try again.
16. Remove the plastic from the vinyl.
17. Take one last pass with the iron to make sure the vinyl has properly adhered.

Etched Glass

The process of creating an etched glass item follows along closely to creating and using a stencil. In fact, the process is identical until the final application of a paint or other substance, in this case, an etching cream, to the surface of the project. A simple pattern is probably the best design for etching because of the cream.

Once the design is selected, print the image onto vinyl. Stencil vinyl is ideal for this because it is made to have the backing stay intact during the cutting process.

Other vinyl can be used; however, results may vary greater because of the different thicknesses of different types of vinyl. Whatever vinyl is chosen, make sure to do a test cut before cutting on the final vinyl to make sure the design is the way you want it.

Before telling the machine to cut the design into the vinyl, make the "Kiss Cut" adjustments for the type of Cricut machine you have. A "Kiss Cut" refers to the desired outcome of the vinyl. The ideal cut will be only through the vinyl, leaving the back paper intact. The following "Kiss Cut" guide can assist in making the right adjustments to the machine before cutting;

- Cricut Explore: Adjust the Smart Dial to "Custom" and select "Stencil Vinyl- 0.2 mm (Cricut)" from the list of materials created custom for Cricut and Explore machines.
- Cricut Mini: #3 blade depth, #2 pressure, high speed, 1 multi-cut, regular blade assembly.
- Cricut Imagine: #3 blade depth, #3 pressure, high speed, 1 multi-cut, regular blade assembly.
- Circuit Expression 2: #4 blade depth, #3 pressure, high speed, 1 multi-cut, regular blade assembly.
- Cricut Expression: #3 blade depth, medium pressure, high speed, 1 multi-cut, and regular blade assembly.
- Cricut Create: #3 blade depth, medium pressure, high speed, 1 multi-cut, and regular blade assembly.

Also, before cutting, load a strip of vinyl with the backing still attached to the cutting mat. When the cutting is finished, remove the unwanted pieces still remaining from the cut by using a "Weeding" hook. After, cut off the excess vinyl.

Remove the backing from the vinyl and adhere it to the project, sealing it firmly to the surface of the project and rubbing it in circular motions to remove air bubbles. Most etching creams require it to be stirred well before application.

Apply a thick coat with a brush with a foam tip rather than bristles to avoid streaking. Follow the directions of the etching cream chosen, but many types will provide a drying time for the product. When the drying time has been exceeded, and the project appears to be ready, rinse the project and brush off the remaining etching cream. Because it is wet the etching may not be as noticeable. Once dry it should become apparent.

Etching can be done to almost any smooth surface, like glass or metal; however, read the etching cream's list of recommended materials if it is provided on the packaging or container.

Wooden Sign

You can add virtually any feature to a piece of wood to create your own sign.
All you need is:

- Your Sign Design – It can be a phrase or an image.
- Vinyl – you can choose the color
- Transfer tape
- Cricut tools kit
- Your wood backing

Step 1

The first step is to prepare the wood. How far you go with this will depend on what type of finished product you are after.

If you want the wood to be rough, then you just need to cut it to shape with a jigsaw.

If you're looking for a smooth finish, then you need to sand it several times first. You may also want to varnish or paint the wood.

Step 2

You can now design your phrase or image on Cricut design space. You need to make sure it is the right size for your wood!

It is important to tell the machine to cut out white space between any letters; you only want the words.

If the writing is bigger than your cutting mat you need to include an easy to cut break point. An alternative color square is usually a good option.

Step 3

Print the phrase or image on your cricut machine. It will advise you if more material needs to be added.

You'll need to use your weeding tool to make sure the edges are exactly how you want them.

Step 4

Carefully apply transfer tape to the other side of your letters. The letters should be lined up exactly how you want them to look on the sign.

You can then peel off the backing and he letters should stay attached to the transfer tape.

Then you should be able to apply this directly to the wood. The transfer tape should come off; leaving the letters stuck to your wood.

That's it; all you have to do now is hang it!

Nail Art

You'll need:

- Vinyl
- Nail polish – your color of choice
- Top coat – to make the polish and nail art last longer.

Step 1
Again you need to take a look at the Cricut Design Space and create the design that you want to appear on your nails.
There is virtually no limit to the design you can create!

Step 2

Place a piece of vinyl into your cricut machine and send the design to the machine. It will cut the intricate shapes for you. You need to make sure they are the right size for your nails.

Step 3

You could use a glue to attach the vinyl but this could leave you in a mess!

Start by placing the design on your nail and removing any excess vinyl.

You can then paint over it with your top coat. This will hold the vinyl in place.

The alternative is to hold the design in place and paint the nail a different color. The design will be left unpainted; all you have to do is carefully remove the vinyl. Again, a top coat should be added to protect the art on your nail.

Thank You Card

If you fancy creating a really personal thank you card, then this is the way to do it.

You'll need:

- Cardboard
- Cricut Pen – this will enable you to write professionally on the card.

Step 1
Again you'll need to access Design Space to find the perfect design for your thank you card. There are hundreds to choose from or you can create your own image and message.

Step 2
Send your design to the Cricut machine and make sure your cardboard is in the machine. Your machine will cut it effortlessly for you.

There is a feature in Design Space that allows you to write and cut. If you activate this you'll be able to write your message directly onto the card and the machine will cut as you go. This allows you to add it to the card you are creating and make it look like 3D.

The machine does the cutting for you so you don't need to worry if you are pressing hard enough.

Step 3
Your design may need a secondary layer to create the right effect. The machine will tell you when to change the material. All you need to do is slide the two pieces together at the end.

Coloring Pages

Adult coloring books have become extremely popular. They are a great way to relax and remove some of the stress of everyday life. However, you don't need to buy them!

It is very easy to make them with your cricut machine.

You'll need:

- Paper or a card
- Cricut Pen – as explained above
- Standard grip cutting mat

Step 1

Go into the Design Space app and select the 'insert shapes' option. You'll need to insert a shape that is the same size as your finished coloring page. You can always start small and create a bigger one on your second attempt.

Step 2

Now click on the 'insert images' button and find anything that you would like to make a coloring sheet.

You'll need to click on it to select it and add it to your design.

You can add more than one image if you wish.

Step 3

Now click the image and select the 'ungroup' option. You can then select each element and change it from scissors to pen. This means it will not be cut out.

You'll then need to regroup all the pieces.

Step 4

Once you're happy with the finished look you can send it to your cricut machine. It will print it and cut the outline at the same time.

Gift Tags

This is actually very similar to creating a thank you card, but on a smaller scale. The great thing about doing this on the cricut is that you can create virtually any design. A printer will only allow you to print a flat image.

You'll need

- Card
- Selection of cricut pens
- Standard grip mat

Step 1

The first thing is to enter the Design Space app and choose the image or images you wish to display on your gift tag.

As part of this you'll need to decide what colors each part of your image should be.

Step 2

Send the image to your cricut machine. Don't forget to add a small hole where the ribbon will go through.

A nice touch is to print letters or an image separately. Design Space can help you to create these and add tabs that will help you to either stick them to the gift tag or hook them into it.

Step 3

Now all you need to do is join the pieces together. You can use your weeding tool to tidy up any difficult areas.

The draw layers can drastically improve the look of your gift tag. You can also add glitter to the finished article to add an extra effect.

A Table Lamp

This is a slightly more adventurous project but still possible for the novice with their cricut machine. It can make a great feature or a gift.

You'll need:

- A lamp; you're not making the actually electric part!
- Adhesive vinyl
- Transfer Tape

Step 1

Go into Design Space and select a design that you like. Don't forget that it needs to let some light through; a completely black lightshade will not give a great effect!

You need to select a piece of vinyl that fits your lampshade. This will give you the dimensions you need when creating your image.

Step 2

Slide your vinyl into the cricut machine and then send the image to be cut. This may take a few minutes depending on the intricacy of your design!

Step 3

You can now remove the vinyl and carefully weed the fabric to ensure the design is completely removed from the backing piece.

Take your time with this, ideally you don't want to do it a second time!

Step 4

Carefully clean the surface of your lamp. It needs to be free of dust, grease and to be fully dry before you can add your vinyl.

Step 5

Apply the transfer tape to your vinyl image. Carefully remove the backing and use the transfer tape to hold the image together as you move it across to your lampshade.

This will need to be reversed if you have added words into your design. If you don't the words will be backwards!

Step 6

Rub the adhesive vinyl gently to ensure it is fully stuck to your lampshade. You can then remove the transfer tape and enjoy the finished lamp.

Note: Don't directly stick it directly on your lightbulb. It will burn!

Xmas Decoration

It's never too early to be thinking about Christmas or Thanksgiving! Your cricut can help you make the best and most unique decorations you've ever had.

You'll need:

- Card
- Adhesive vinyl
- Adhesive foil
- Cricut pens

Step 1

Locate your desired image in Design Space or draw / write your own using the cricut pen.

It is a good idea to use a layered effect to create a more interesting decoration. You can even opt to use different materials for each layer. The app will guide you through the necessary steps.

For example, you can write a message in black on white card and have the machine cut it out. This can then be adhered to a red card cut into a shape by your machine.

Step 2

Add some images and writing on foil to improve the overall effect of your decoration and then adhere them to a piece of vinyl. Make sure the image is evenly placed.

Step 3

The vinyl can be hung to create an enticing effect. However, you can also purchase clear plastic baubles and stick the adhesive vinyl to them. You'll need to use transfer tape to achieve the right result.

This is one project that improves with experimentation!

Wall Art

If you can't afford your own Picasso or Van Gogh then you may be interested in creating your own wall art. It's not as difficult as it sounds!

You'll need:

- A wood frame or some wood to make your own
- Stapler
- Canvas

Step 1
Measure the size of your frame and add one inch to the measurements. This is the size of your canvas you need. If you're making your own frame, then you can select the size of your image.

Step 2

Go into Design Space and choose an image you like. You'll need to create a blank space first the same size as the inside of your frame, not your canvas piece.

You can then insert your image into this space.

Step 3

As before you'll need to ungroup the image and change each element to pen instead of scissors. Unless your image is supposed to have sections cut out in which case leave them as scissors.

This can actually be a good way of creating layers and altering the final appeal of your art.

Step 4

Now print your work of art onto the canvas, using your cricut machine to get the lines right.

This canvas can then be wrapped round your frame and stapled to the inside of your frame to hold it taut.

If you're making your own frame, you can adhere the canvas to the wood and glue the wood together to create the same level of tautness.

Now hang you work of art and admire!

Cupcake Wrappers

This is a great project to do with the children or just for a themed party. It will help to set just the right image for your guests!

You'll need:

- Paper of a card
- That's it!

Step 1

Take a look at the Design Space site and select the design or designs that appeal to you the most. The great thing about these designs is that you can create more than you need and save the extra for another occasion.

Your image will need to be approximately 9 inches long to wrap round a standard cupcake.

Step 2

Load your card in the machine and send the image or images. Within a few minutes they should all be printed and cut.

Step 3

Wrap the card round your cupcake and clip it together by making a small incision in each end. If you've used an actual cupcake design from Design Space the tab will already be present.

An alternative is to overlap the end and use a dot of glue to hold the two ends together.

Top Tip: When doing a children's party you can actually create the designs and get the children to decorate them before you wrap them round the cup cakes.

Jam Jar Labels

If you, or some that you know, loves to make jam then this is the perfect gift to make them smile. It is also very easy to make!

You'll need:

- Adhesive Vinyl
- Weeding Tool
- Transfer Tape
- Jam Jars

Step 1

You need to prep your jars by cleaning them thoroughly. This will ensure the vinyl sticks properly. It is also important to measure the size of your jam jars; this is the height and width you have available for your cricut labels.

Step 2

Go into Design Space. You'll probably find that the jam or spice name you need is already there. Of course you can design your own or use images instead.

Select the image you desire then select the detach option in actions. This prevents cricut from relocating the name to where it will fit best when printed.

Don't forget to select your preferred font and resize the letters to your desired size.

Step 3

Once you have all the names and images laid out you can go back into the actions tab and select attach. This will lock them into the position you have chosen.

You can now send the file to your cricut machine.

Step 4

Use your weeding tool to get perfect edges as you remove all the words from the vinyl. Once you are happy with how they look apply the transfer tape and slowly peel the backing off.

The transfer tape will hold it in place as you stick the letters to your clean jam jars. Once they are stuck you can remove the transfer tape and congratulate yourself on some fine looking jam jar labels.

The Chore Chart

If you're looking for something a little different and more challenging, then the chore chart is the right project for you.

It's also a great way for your children to monitor their chores and which ones still need doing!

You'll need:

- Metal Board
- Cricut chore chart cartridge. This is not essential but will make it easier.
- Magnets
- Adhesive vinyl
- Transfer Tape

Step 1
The first thing you need to do is verify that your magnets stick to your metal board! You can then measure the surface area of your magnets; this is the size your print will need to be.
It is also important to make sure the magnets are clean and ready for the adhesive vinyl.

Step 2
The next step is to go into Design Space and look at the different images available. You'll need to select an image for every chore that you or your child is likely to do.
Position them carefully on the screen to optimize your use of your adhesive vinyl.

Step 3
Don't forget to create a name in Vinyl. You can use Design Space to make individual letters or join the name together.
Once this is done you will need to print it all onto your vinyl.

Step 4
Carefully remove all the letters and images. It is likely that the weeding tool will be useful at this stage.
Take your time as one slip can destroy your efforts!

Step 5

Stick the transfer tape to the front of all the letters and images. Then peel the adhesive backing off and stick the vinyl images to the front of the magnets.

Make sure there are no bubbles in the vinyl before you remove the transfer tape.

Now you just need to introduce the concept to your child(ren)!

Drinks Coasters

This is a delightful project which can help you to personalize your home. It can even be good as a gift. The beauty of creating cricut coasters is that you can actually encompass personal memories if you wish.

You'll need:

- Cork
- Adhesive Vinyl
- Adhesive Felt
- Transfer Tape

Step 1

Decide how many coasters you would like to make, how big they should be and what shape you want them. They do not need to be circular! A star, square or even an irregular shape can be just as effective!

Step 2

Create this shape in your Design Space and allow the cricut machine to cut your design into the cork.

Step 3

Now you need to select the image you wish to print on each coaster. You can even choose different ones for each coaster.
Instead of an image you can opt for a monogram or even a phrase or date that reminds you of a special occasion.
These will need to be the same size as your coaster.

Use the cricut machine to cut these shapes into the adhesive vinyl. This can then be transferred to the cork using transfer tape; as described previously.
Make sure there are no bubbles in your vinyl as you apply it.

Step 4

You can now add felt to the bottom to help protect your furniture or even add small pieces of felt to the top; to improve the look.

This step is not essential, it will depend on your design and whether you feel felt is beneficial to help protect your furniture.

Baby Blanket

This can be a great keepsake for the future, a useful daily item or even a unique and special gift. In fact, it doesn't have to be just for your baby. You can make one of these blankets for virtually any occasion.

You'll need:

- Cricut machine
- Iron
- Iron-on fabric
- Standard cotton fabric or plain blanket – any color

Step 1

Go into the Design Space app and select the numbers or test you wish to add to your blanket. You'll need to remove any negative spaces and reverse the letters and numbers. This is so that when they are stuck to your blanket they can be read properly.

You can choose a date of birth, a short phrase or even a picture. There is practically no limit to how many shapes you can create; as long as they'll fit on the blanket.

Step 2

Now you need to use your cricut machine to print and cut each letter and number onto your iron-on fabric. These should be ready to use as soon as they are printed,
You can then place them on your blanket and iron them into position.

The key here is to have a flat surface and then place a folded towel onto it. The blanket can go on top. This will allow your fabric to have a little flex which will ensure the edge of the images is stuck properly.

When ironing on the fabric you need to ensure the temperature is at least 305° Fahrenheit. Hold the iron over the image for approximately 30 seconds to ensure it sticks properly.

A Bookmark

The bookmark is actually a very simple project but it makes a perfect gift and a useful item even in the digital age.
You'll need:

- Vinyl
- Paper of card

Step 1
Open your Design Space and create a new shape. It is best to start with a rectangle approximately 6 inches tall by 1.5 inches wide.
Inside this rectangle you'll need to place your text. You can write any short phrase you want or even add a picture.

Step 2
Go into the settings and make sure that the text is set as a separate layer and then click attach. You can then send the file to your machine and it will cut the phrase out of your vinyl rectangle.

The result is a stylish book mark with the words cut into it. It's that simple!

It is a good idea to then laminate the bookmarks as this will protect them and help them to last for longer.

The Unicorn Mask

These instructions are for a unicorn mask but they can easily be adapted to any other image.

This makes it perfect for children's parties and even for those themed adult parties.

You'll need:

- Cricut machine
- Felt – various colors
- Fabric Glue
- Scissors

Step 1
You'll need to find a mask image of your unicorn or other animal. This is not something that already exists in Design Space. You have to locate one and upload it to your Cricut Design Space.

You may need to resize the image according to the size of your head or that of your child's.

Step 2
You can choose any colors you want for the different parts of the unicorn mask. By pressing "make it" the cricut will print the different colors, cutting in the process.

Step 3
You can now assemble the parts of the mask, the guide on Design Space should help to ensure you get this part right. You can opt to use fabric glue for this or you can use adhesive fabric and transfer tape to get the different layers together.

It is also important to add two holes to your mask. One should be on each side of the mask to allow the ribbon to be threaded through. This is important to ensure the mask can be properly secured.

It is also possible to add to the design by using glitter, sequins or embroidering a pattern into it. The choice is yours!

Tips and Techniques

While the Cricut's website offers a myriad of tips and techniques, there are some tried-and-true ways of using your machine and saving money and time. Use this chapter to get out-of-the-box ideas and tips for troubleshooting your machine.

10 Top Tips and Tactics for success:

1. Freezer paper is ideal for creating custom stencils.
2. Label blades for use on paper, vinyl, fabric, etc. and only use those blades on that medium. This helps preserve the lifetime of the blades.
3. Learn the proper cutting methods and approved materials by reading the cutting guide on Cricut.com.
4. Spray paint is a great tool for coloring vinyl if ever in a pinch and do not have a required color on hand or the time for it to arrive.
5. Free fonts can be uploaded and used in the Cricut Design Space. Find free fonts on websites such as dafont.com, fontsquirrel.com, or 1001freefonts.com.
6. Personal images and pictures can be used for Cricut projects if the image is saved on the computer as a PNG, JPG, or SCG.
7. Test out materials before printing and cutting a final project to be sure it will work as planned.
8. Pens other than Cricut pens work with the machine. Some brands to try include Sharpie, American Crafts, and Recollections.
9. Avoid paper curling by pulling the cutting mat from the project and not the other way around.

10. Lint rollers are great for removing leftover materials from cutting mats. If the mats need further cleaning, use soap and water and gently rub clean with soft cloth. Rinse with clean water and let air dry.

Cutting with your Cricut

Masking tape or painter's tape is great to place on the edges of materials when they are not sticking well to the cutting mat.

Thick cuts sometimes will not be cut completely through. To avoid having to do it by hand, keep the material in place when it is finished cutting the first cut without pressing the arrows button to remove it, and cut it again by selecting the "Go" or "C" button.

Print and Cut

An ink jet printer works best for printing. A laser printer sometimes heats the toner too high, which makes it hard for the Cricut machine to read.

Internet Explorer or Safari is best for working with large images because these browsers support images up to about 9 inches high and about 6 inches wide. Chrome and Firefox cap their heights around 8 inches high and about 5 inches wide.

A white paper is best for printing the registration marks for projects. If the project is any other color, print and cut on white paper first and then attach them to the colored paper before putting it into the Cricut.

Writing with your Cricut

Pens work best when stored cap-side down. This keeps the ink at the tip.

Thin pens can have their barrel widened by winding tape around it. Electrical or painter's tape works well and does not leave a sticky residue behind.

Scoring with your Cricut

Folding materials is made easier with the use of the scoring tool when it is placed in the pen holder in the machine.

Deepen the score lines in a custom design by doubling up the score lines on the canvas in the Design Space.

Embossing with your Cricut

It can be done! Use the accessory adapter in the place of the blade housing and insert the scoring stylus into it. When the Cricut is then told to cut, it will instead emboss.

Blades for your Cricut

Sharpen blades with aluminum foil by cutting a basic design into the foil when it is on the cutting mat.

Designing for your Cricut

Firefox and Safari are best for using Design Space. Google Chrome does not work well with it.

Save the free designs Design Space offers by saving a new project with the design and name it with a description of the design for easy access later on.

Cut the canvas exactly how it is laid out by selecting "All" and clicking on "Attach." This ensures everything stays where they were placed without the machine defaulting to individual cuts.

Instructional handbooks are available for Cricut Access members. This link is a functional place to learn how to assemble cartridges. (www.home.cricut.com/handbooks)

Cut the largest layer last to avoid the material from moving around during the later smaller cuts. This means placing the largest layer as the topmost layer and the finer elements at the bottom in Design Space.

Cricut Mats
Disinfectant wipes by Lysol or Clorox can be used to help mats regain their stickiness.

Duct tape can be applied to the underside of the mat if a cut goes too deep and slices through.

Rotate the mat by turning it around to the other side to even out the cut marks on it. This is especially useful if a cutting path is being worn into the mat from cutting the same design multiple times.

12"X24" mats can be cut in two to make two 12"X12" mats.

Materials
You can problably save money by buying your materials online.

Sign shops in the community may also be willing to give vinyl scraps out for free if asked.

Colored cardstock that is not available can be replicated by printing the color desired onto white cardstock and then used in the project in place of the colored one.

Toilet paper or paper towel rolls are excellent storage tools for rolls of vinyl. This prevents them from unrolling and becoming ruined in improper storage.

Contact paper that is clear can remove vinyl from its backing smoothly.

Weeding
Safety pins are excellent tools for removing intricate pieces. Headlamps with an LED light or a sunny window are good, inexpensive tools for seeing the lines while weeding. For more of an investment, consider purchasing a lightbox with an LED light or the Cricut BrightPad.

Assembly of Projects
Foam mounts that self-adhere or glued bits of foam board or cardboard can be applied in between layers to make them stand out slightly.

A fast drying and sticky glue is ideal for putting projects together. Consider glue made especially for the materials being used, like paper glues or fabric glues. Tacky glues are good options because they allow some ease of movement but typically take longer to dry.

Troubleshooting

The incorrect cartridge name appears on the Cricut screen
Follow the following steps to correct the error:

1. Sometimes in manufacturing, the cartridge stickers are placed on backward on the cartridge. Take out the inserted cartridge and reinsert it backward to check if this is the problem. If this does not solve the problem, move to the next step.
2. Does this happen with all cartridges?
   a) Yes- Move to the next step
   b) No- Call customer service or chat online with customer service if it still displays the wrong name after putting it in backward.
3. Hard reset may be required at this point. Follow the directions in the user manual for this. Again, if this does not fix the problem move to the next step.
4. Update Firmware, especially if it is not up to date. If this does not fix the problem, move to the next step.
5. Call customer service or chat online with customer service if none of the above steps solved the problem.

When images are added to the queue the Cricut machine freezes

Before selecting the image keys, always select the gray feature keys.

Follow the following steps to correct the error if it is still occurring:

1. Turn off the Cricut and let it rest for up to one hour. Let it rest for at least a minimum of 10 minutes.
2. Double check how the characters were entered. Try re-entering the characters in the accurate order and allowing the image to show up on the screen before keying in the subsequent character.
3. "Characters won't fit" appears when the image memory is exceeded in the queue. Try removing images to see if the problem is fixed. If the problem continues, proceed to the next step.
4. If you insert another cartridge, does this error still occur?
   a) YES- Move to the next step.
   b) NO- Call customer service or chat online customer service to speak with them about the error.
5. Hard reset may be required at this point. Follow the directions in the user manual for this. Again, if this does not fix the problem move to the next step.
6. Update Firmware, especially if it is not up to date. If this does not fix the problem, move to the next step.
7. Call customer service or chat online with customer service if none of the above steps solved the problem.

The Cricut Machine keypad has glitches

There are two common keyboard errors that occur; the buttons do not respond when pressed and none of the buttons will work despite lights being lit on the keyboard. If this does not explain your problem, call customer service or chat online with customer service about the problem. If your error is one of the two most common problems, follow the steps below for whichever your problem is.

Non-responsive buttons when pressed:

1. Check that the machine recognizes the inserted cartridge by making sure the screen displays the cartridges name. If this does not fix the problem, move to the next step.
2. Check that the mat is loaded into the machine properly. If this does not fix the problem, move to the next step.
3. If you insert another cartridge, does this error still occur?
   a) YES- Move to the next step.
   b) NO- Call customer service or chat online customer service to speak with them about the error.
4. Hard reset may be required at this point. Follow the directions in the user manual for this. Again, if this does not fix the problem move to the next step.
5. Update Firmware, especially if it is not up to date. If this does not fix the problem, move to the next step.
6. Call customer service or chat online with customer service if none of the above steps solved the problem.

No buttons will respond despite lights coming on:

1. Update Firmware, especially if it is not up to date. Lights on the left side of the keyboard, the power button, and the cut button will light up when in Firmware mode. If this does not fix the problem, move to the next step.
2. Call customer service or chat online with customer service if the above step did not solve the problem.

Unloading or loading the mat makes the Cricut machine freeze

Follow the following steps to correct the error:

1. Turn off the Cricut and let it rest for up to one hour. Let it rest for at least a minimum of 10 minutes.
2. Did you switch a cartridge while the machine was on? This is called "hot swapping" and can result in the machine freezing.
3. YES- Turn off your machine and switch the cartridge. If this does not solve the problem, move to the next step.
4. NO- Move to the next step.
5. If you insert another cartridge, does this error still occur?
   a) YES- Move to the next step.
   b) NO- Call customer service or chat online customer service to speak with them about the error.
6. Hard reset may be required at this point. Follow the directions in the user manual for this. Again, if this does not fix the problem move to the next step.
7. Update Firmware, especially if it is not up to date. If this does not fix the problem, move to the next step.
8. Call customer service or chat online with customer service if none of the above steps solved the problem.

During cutting the carriage does not travel along the track

Follow the following steps to correct the error:

1. Can the carriage car move easily to the right and left while the machine is on?
   a) YES- Move to the next step.
   b) NO- Call customer service or chat online customer service to speak with them about the problem.
2. Look carefully at the belt, roller bars, and carriage car to see if any damage is evident. Take photos of any observed damage and Call customer service or chat online customer service to speak with them about the problem.
   a) Belt- Is it lose or broken?
   h) Carriage car- Is it on the track? Is it on the track straight?
3. Call customer service or chat online customer service to speak with them about the problem is no damage is obvious.

When loaded into the Cricut machine the mat becomes crooked

Do not hold the corners or sides of the may when loading it. Instead, hold the bottom in the center and position the mat slightly under and against the roller bar's rubber rings. This is easiest when the bottom of the mat is lifted up gently.
Follow the following steps to correct the error:

1. Look carefully at the roller bar to see if any damage is evident. Take photos of any observed damage and Call customer service or chat online customer service to speak with them about the problem. If there is no damage noticeable, move on to the next step.
2. The correct mat size must be used for the machine. Double check it is correct. If this does not fix the problem, move on to the next step.
3. Before loading the mat, make sure it is aligned with guides, and the mat's edges are below the roller bar. If this does not fix the problem, move on to the next step.
4. As the roller bar begins to roll, lightly press the mat underneath with gentle pressure.
5. Call customer service or chat online with customer service if none of the above steps solved the problem.

During cutting the machine freezes

Follow the following steps to correct the error:

1. Turn off the Cricut and let it rest for up to one hour. Let it rest for at least a minimum of 10 minutes.
2. If you insert another cartridge, does this error still occur?
   a) YES- Move to the next step.
   b) NO- Call customer service or chat online customer service to speak with them about the error.
3. Hard reset may be required at this point. Follow the directions in the user manual for this. Again, if this does not fix the problem move to the next step.
4. Update Firmware, especially if it is not up to date. If this does not fix the problem, move to the next step.
5. Call customer service or chat online with customer service if none of the above steps solved the problem

Conclusion

Thanks for making it through to the end of Cricut Project Ideas: A Beginners Guide to Mastering Your Cricut Machine, let's hope it was informative and able to provide you with all of the tools you need to achieve your creative goals.

The next step is to get crafting! Enjoy your new knowledge of your amazing machine and give a new project a try. If you are about to start your first project, consider trying one of the beginner projects outlined in the previous chapters. For those that have a few cuts under their belt, give one of the alternative projects a try! Have fun and do not limit yourself. The beauty of the Cricut is the versatility of functions and user-friendly format. Use this to make your life and home and those of your friends and family more exciting and designed!

If at any point you get stumped on how to use your machine or are wondering what materials you should use, reference the previous chapters or visit cricut.com for help. Understanding and reviewing the foundations of your Cricut is wise to make sure you are building on your skills with a solid foundation of knowledge. From there your creativity can blossom, and the sky is the limit for what you can create. So now, stop reading and start doing! Make your first t-shirt design or hanging planter and enjoy your creations.

Finally, if you found this book useful in any way, a review on Amazon is always appreciated!

~ Notes ~

....

....

....

....

....

....

....

....

....

....

....

....

....

....

91087565R00064

Made in the USA
Middletown, DE
28 September 2018